Charleston
SOUTH CAROLINA

A PHOTOGRAPHIC PORTRAIT

PHOTOGRAPHY BY
Rick Rhodes

NARRATIVE BY
Michelle Salater

First published in the United States of America by:

Twin Lights Publishers, Inc.
8 Hale Street
Rockport, Massachusetts 01966
Telephone: (978) 546-7398
http://www.twinlightspub.com

ISBN: 978-1-885435-94-1
ISBN: 1-885435-94-0

10 9 8 7 6 5 4 3

Boone Hall Plantation *(opposite)*

Live oaks planted in 1743 line the plantation entrance, making it one of the world's longest oak-lined avenues.

(frontispiece)

Morris Island Lighthouse

(jacket front)

Drayton Hall

(jacket back)

Low Country

Book design by:
SYP Design & Production, Inc.
www.sypdesign.com

Printed in China

Charleston defines Southern hospitality. A bustling city with a timeless atmosphere, the historic peninsula has maintained her old-world charm and a distinct culture. Steeped in 300 years of history, it was here, at Fort Moultrie, where patriots won the first decisive battle of the Revolutionary War. A century later, across from Charleston Harbor and the magnificent Battery mansions, the first shot of the Civil War was fired at Fort Sumter. Today, as in centuries past, church steeples dominate the Charleston skyline, hence its nickname, "Holy City." Buildings such as The Old Exchange and U.S. Customs House stand testament that Charleston's architectural beauty has not worn with time. Antebellum homes with sprawling piazzas and delightful gardens tucked behind ornate, wrought iron gates stand as proudly as they did generations ago. Live oaks dripping with Spanish moss continue to line the plantation drives and shade some of the oldest graveyards in the country.

In this genteel city, its people and culture are as colorful as the buildings. The blend of West African, English, Caribbean, French, and German cultural influences are apparent on every street corner. Charlestonians are a proud people who cherish their city and welcome visitors with open arms. A booming metropolis with a multi-billion-dollar tourism industry, Charleston hosts events such as Spoleto and the Cooper River Bridge Run, which draw participants and visitors from around the world. Renowned courses beckon golf aficionados. White beaches and waves of the Atlantic are a favorite for sunbathers and surfers alike.

The images throughout this book capture the soul of Charleston and the beauty of the surrounding Lowcountry: pristine shorelines, picturesque salt marshes, and historic plantations with sprawling gardens. We hope you enjoy this colorful collection by local photographer, Rick Rhodes, and are inspired to visit this city by the sea again and again.

The deSaussure House

A carriage tour stops to admire the deSaussure House verandas and iron balconies, which offer an unsurpassed view of Charleston Harbor and Fort Sumter. Built in the late 1700s and renovated in the 1850s, the home provided the family shelter until the city came under bombardment by Union guns.

Magnolia Plantation House and Gardens *(above and opposite)*

Acquired by the Drayton family in 1676, the Magnolia Plantation grounds and its gardens cover almost 500 acres. When the original house burned, it was rebuilt but later leveled by Union troops. The current manor, built in 1873, is open to the public and furnished with three centuries of Drayton family heirlooms and antiques. Considered America's oldest gardens, with some sections growing since 1680, the plantation features thousands of flowers, including over 900 varieties of camellias. The grounds are as diverse as the year-round blooms, with wetlands, lakes, forests, and marshes to explore.

The Long Bridge, Magnolia Gardens

Reverend John Grimke-Drayton built
the picturesque Long Bridge in the 1840s.
The bridge's arc is divided into three
sections, allowing each to form an oval
image in the lake's reflection. One of
seven bridges on the property, this
simple, white picket bridge is the most
popular.

The Little Dancer

Sculpted by the prominent Charleston artist Willard Hirsch, this children's drinking fountain, *The Little Dancer*, overlooks Charleston Harbor. The 21-inch statue stands in White Point Gardens. The inscription on the back reads, "Given to the children of Charleston by a friend."

Audubon Swamp Garden *(top)*

A newer addition to Magnolia Gardens, the Audubon Swamp Garden is a 60-acre blackwater swamp inhabited by an array of unique flora and fauna. Great blue herons feast among cypress and tupelo gum trees, and egrets and other waterfowl nest within feet of the walking path.

Magnolia Gardens *(bottom)*

Paved bike and walking trails allow visitors to experience the diverse landscape of the plantation. Guided tours are available, from Camellia walks to bird watching. For those who want to rest their feet, tram tours are available and led by a naturalist.

Magnolia Cemetery *(opposite)*

The family of William B. Smith erected this pyramid mausoleum after the banker and self-made millionaire died. Established in 1850, Magnolia Cemetery is the oldest public graveyard in Charleston and is the resting place for many of the city's public officials and prominent citizens.

THEO. P. MOOD.
BORN
MAY 8. 1844
DIED DEC. 13. 1907
FATHER.

Middleton Place

Middleton Place is a well-preserved, 18th-century rice plantation and National Historic Landmark on the Ashley River. Henry Middleton, president of the First Continental Congress, built the enchanting, 65-acre, landscaped garden, the country's oldest. Rolling terraces descend into "The Butterfly Lakes."

Spring Bloom at Middleton Place

Swans swim freely in the glassy waters of the Azalea Pool, which separates the forest from the formal gardens. During the spring, visitors from all over the world come to see the hillsides and embankments explode with colorful azalea blooms.

Angel Oak

The Angel Oak on John's Island was already old when English settlers arrived. "The Tree", which locals call the enormous live oak, stands 65 feet high, has a circumference of 25.5 feet, and is estimated to be over 1,400 years old. Even more impressive is its 17,000-square-foot shaded canopy.

Washington Square

A statue of George Washington is one of many monuments in this live oak-shaded park. Located at the bustling corner of Meeting and Broad Street in the Historic District, Washington Square is a quiet place to stroll or sit peacefully and enjoy the view.

Marion Square (*above*)

The Marion Square fountain is a newer addition to the 10-acre, urban green space. Once used as assembly grounds for the State Arsenal, this square has become a frequent gathering place for locals and visitors who come to view its historical monuments, take a walk, or attend events.

John C. Calhoun Monument (*opposite*)

The statue of South Carolinian John C. Calhoun, renowned orator, U.S. Senator, and Vice President, towers above Marion Square. The monument's cornerstone, laid in 1858, contains Calhoun's last Senate speech, a lock of his hair, a banner from his funeral, and a cannonball from the Revolutionary War Battle of Fort Moultrie.

1782 — 1850
TRVTH JVSTICE
AND THE
CONSTITVTION

Fort Moultrie Monument (opposite)

This centennial tribute to the Revolutionary War defenders of Sullivan's Island was finished a year late, on June 28, 1877. Although the records indicate the bronzed soldier was meant to be generic, many people believe it to be Sergeant William Jasper, famous for retrieving the fort's fallen flag from outside its wall.

Confederate Defenders Monument (above)

This monument, in White Point Gardens, honors the Confederate defenders of Charleston. The bronzed male warrior, with a shield bearing the South Carolina state seal and a female, holding an immortal garland of laurel, represent the City of Charleston. Stars on the base symbolize the 11 Confederate states.

The Keokuk Gun (top)

Confederate troops salvaged this 11-inch Dahlgren Naval Gun from the wreck of the USS *Keokuk*, one of the Federal ironclad ships that attacked Fort Sumter in April 1863. Once raised from the sands of Sullivan's Island, the Confederacy used it to defend the city against Union forces.

The Fort Sumter House (bottom)

The Fort Sumter House, a private condominium residence on The Battery, towers above White Point Gardens and Murray Boulevard. Built in the 1920s as the Fort Sumter Hotel, it was one of the city's most luxurious hotels and catered to prominent guests.

Moultrie Monument

The statue honoring Revolutionary War hero General William Moultrie is the newest monument in White Point Gardens. The bronze overlooks the harbor and Fort Moultrie, site of the June 1776 battle that Moultrie led and where he is now buried.

Waterfront Park Pier

Waterfront Park's 400-foot pier is a family favorite. Lined with plenty of picnic tables and wooden swings under the pavilions, it is the perfect spot to watch the harbor's activities, take shelter from the sun, and cool off with the sea breeze.

Waterfront Park *(top and bottom)*

During the summer months, children and adults alike stay cool splashing in the stately pineapple-shaped fountain and the circular spray fountain in Waterfront Park. Located downtown off East Bay Street, the 8-acre park runs parallel to the entry of Charleston Harbor and is built on remnants of old wharves.

Along with its grand fountains, the park contains "garden rooms", a walking or running path, and benches for sightseers with tired feet.

Fountain Walk *(above)*

Located downtown along Aquarium Wharf, Fountain Walk is a retail and commercial center overlooking the Cooper River. Restaurants, shops, and a fitness studio, as well as the American Military Museum, occupy the space. Charter boat tours, such as the schooner *Pride*, operate from the Fountain Walk dock.

Evening Lights *(opposite)*

Fountain Walk offers breathtaking views of the Ravenel Bridge and the Cooper River, especially at night when the bridge lights reflect off the water.

The Arthur Ravenel Jr. Bridge *(pages 26–27)*

There is nothing more spectacular than the Arthur Ravenel Jr. Bridge at sunset. Built high above the Cooper River to accommodate large container ships, it is the longest cable-stayed bridge in the country. The eight-lane bridge, which has a bike and walking path, opened in July 2005.

Fountain Walk Signs

The ultimate sign for visitors who may lose their sense of where "home" is located may be found on Fountain Walk by the South Carolina Aquarium, with the Ravenel Bridge in the background.

Charleston County Courthouse

The County Courthouse, built in 1792, proudly sits northwest of the intersection known as the Four Corners of Law. In 1989, Hurricane Hugo swept through the city, leaving the courthouse in shambles, but the Historic Charleston Foundation and concerned citizens helped rebuild and restore the magnificent building.

The Old Exchange *(above)*

The Old Exchange is one of the three most historically significant buildings of Colonial America. Since 1680, a public building has stood in this spot, although the British erected the current building in 1771. From its steps in 1776, South Carolina publicly declared itself an independent colony.

The United States Custom House *(opposite)*

The grandiose Customs House, fashioned in the Roman Corinthian order, overlooks East Bay Street. Designed by one of America's most prominent architects, Ammi B. Young, the interior is impressive, with marble used throughout and ceilings stenciled in patriotic motifs. Construction was completed in 1879.

California Dreaming (top)

Accessible by land or boat, this fort-like restaurant and bar along the Ashley River provides every table with a lovely view of Charleston Harbor. This family-friendly establishment serves everything from steak and seafood, to Mexican cuisine.

Ashley River Bridge (bottom)

The Ashley River Bridge crosses the beautiful Ashley River, linking the historic downtown peninsula with James Island and other communities west of the river. Each year, thousands participate in the 10k James Island Connector Run, in which runners begin from downtown and run over the bridge and back.

City Hall (opposite)

This elegant Adam-style building with marble trim, designed by Gabriel Manigualt, was originally constructed for The First Bank of the United States. The bank's charter was revoked in 1811, and the building became City Hall in 1818. It sits at the intersection of Broad and Meeting, known as the Four Corners of Law.

Fort Moultrie *(top and bottom)*

In its 171-year history, Fort Moultrie, on Sullivan's Island, defended Charleston twice. During the Revolutionary War, the original palmetto fort, commanded by William Moultrie, drove off the British Navy after a nine-hour battle. A century later, the fort was bombarded for almost two years by Federal forces and left in shambles. The third fort, built in 1809, stands today and has been restored. Visitors learn about the fort's history, from the Revolution to WWII, and see the typical weapons from those different periods.

Sullivan's Island

The aerial view of Sullivan's Island shows some of the Charleston area's most spectacular seaside homes, from modern to surviving 19th-century beach houses. This quiet, mainly residential area is one of Mount Pleasant's three barrier islands.

Fort Sumter *(top and bottom)*

On April 12, 1861, the War Between the States began when Confederate gunners surrounded Fort Sumter and fired. Thirty-four hours later, Federal troops surrendered. The pentagon-shaped fort was integeral to Charleston's defense, and the Confederacy controlled it from 1861 to 1865. During that time, it experienced heavy bombardment, and beginning August 1863, it came under one of the longest sieges in history, lasting 587 days. Today, tour boats take visitors to the national monument where they are free to explore the ruins. The ride provides a spectacular view of Charleston as well as a narrated history of the harbor.

Fort Sumter National Monument

An impressive museum tells the history of Fort Sumter through original artifacts, photographs, and interactive displays. On display is the 33-star garrison flag that flew over the fort on April 12, 1861. The National Park Service has rangers available to answer questions.

The Old Slave Mart Museum *(above)*

Now a museum chronicling the city's African-American experience, slave auctions were held in what was called the shed from 1856 until 1863. Once part of a series of buildings on Chalmers Street, only the Slave Mart remains, making it the only known existing building in South Carolina used as a slave auction.

The Pink House *(opposite)*

Built in the 1690s within the walled city of Charles Towne, the city's oldest stone house derives its name from Bermuda stone, a naturally pink soft coral. The 17 Chalmers Street house claims to be the oldest tavern in the South, as it was originally a tavern and bordello for sailors. Today, it is home to an art gallery.

The Pineapple House Gates *(top)*

The famous stone Pineapple Gates on Chalmers Street were molded to resemble Italian pinecones. Pineapple moldings and carvings, symbols of hospitality, are found on gateposts, doorways, and walls throughout Charleston. During colonial times, their rarity made them a status symbol.

Battery Home *(botom)*

This gorgeous home overlooking White Point Gardens was built in the mid-19th century. Located at 26 South Battery, the Italianate-style architecture was a reaction to the formal classicism of the previous century.

South Carolina Society Hall *(opposite)*

The Society's headquarters, constructed in 1804, is a stunning Adam-style building designed by architect and member, Gabriel Manigualt. The porch and Ionic pillars were added in 1825. Organized in 1737 by French Huguenot businessmen, the association built schools for orphans and now donates college scholarships.

Nathaniel Russell House (opposite, top, and bottom)

Recognized as one of America's most important neoclassical dwellings, the 51 Meeting Street mansion was built for shipping merchant Nathaniel Russell and his wife. The 71-year-old Russell supposedly spent $80,000 on its construction, which was completed in 1808. The elaborate interior showcases the geometrically shaped rooms furnished with English, French, and Charleston period antiques, rare china, and historical paintings. Most impressive is the free-flying stairway, which soars three flights without any noticeable support. This grand National Historic Landmark and its gardens are open daily for tours.

Murray Boulevard *(above and opposite)*

Elegant homes along Murray Boulevard enjoy the ocean breeze and the view. The extended seawall from White Point Gardens along the Ashley River is credited to Charleston businessman Andrew Buist Murray for whom the boulevard is named. He encouraged the city to fill 50 acres of mudflats and marshes, and the project was completed in 1911. Today, the homes in this area are quite diverse, although most along Murray Boulevard are Georgian style, much like those along White Point Gardens.

Rainbow Row (*above*)

The postcard-famous Rainbow Row
derives its name from the vibrantly colorful houses lining East Bay Street. Built
in the mid-to-late 1700s as merchants'
stores and homes, these now-private
residences delight visitors and residents
with their purple, salmon, yellow, olive,
and pink facades.

Two Meeting Street Inn (*opposite*)

Tucked behind wrought iron gates, Two
Meeting Street is Charleston's oldest inn.
Rocking chairs on the arched piazzas
allow guests a panoramic view of The
Battery. This 1890s Queen Anne mansion
was originally a private residence, a
wedding present from merchant George
Williams to his daughter, Martha.

32 South Battery Home *(opposite)*

Completed in 1782 for Colonel John Ashe, this grand, two-tiered piazza home on South Battery faces White Point Gardens. The home is widely recognizable by its prominent cupola.

187 Wentworth Street *(above)*

An historic Wentworth Street home, built circa 1822, was once owned by Thomas Lee, the grandfather of the youngest Lieutenant General of the Confederacy, Stephen Dill Lee. The piazza, typical of many Charleston homes, overlooks a pond and two gardens, one of which is covered in Crepe Myrtles.

The William Roper House *(above)*

This monumental East Battery home, with its two-story-high Ionic columns and arched terrace, is a perfect example of 19th-century Greek Revival architecture. Built in 1838 by Robert William Roper, a well-known cotton planter, the piazza stretches the length of the lot and boasts the best ocean view in Charleston.

The Porcher-Simonds House *(opposite)*

Cotton broker Francis J. Porcher had this impressive 29 East Battery mansion built in 1856. John C. Simonds purchased it in the early 1890s and remodeled it in the Italian Renaissance Revival style, adding the square and oval double porticos and a semi-oval wing.

Battery Carriage House Inn

This cozy bed-and-breakfast with a European ambiance offers ten rooms and one suite. Silver-service continental breakfast is served in the rooms or in the garden, under the rose arbor. Its ideal location at 20 South Battery is a short walking distance to shops, restaurants, and attractions.

The Palmer Home

Built in 1848 by John Ravenel, The Pink Palace is one of the most prominent mansions on The Battery. This Italianate-style house, furnished with 200-year-old antiques, is a bed-and-breakfast with four guest rooms and a separate carriage house. The piazza offers guests a magnificent harbor view and a cool ocean breeze.

The Nathanial Russell Middleton House

Completed in 1858 for planter Nathanial Russell Middleton, this Italianate-style pink home is located at one of the most prestigious addresses in the city. During construction, the eastern wall of the home next door, 24 South Battery, had to be torn down to accommodate this 22 South Battery mansion.

Battery Home Cupola

Legend has it that the cupola on John Ashe's 32 South Battery home was once used as a lighthouse for ships entering Charleston Harbor. No one has been able to prove or disprove this claim.

South Battery Home *(above)*

Shutters adorn most of Charleston's historic houses. Decorative yet functional, they provided protection against sun, hurricanes, and intruders. In the 18th century, paneled shutters were located on the first floor while windows on the floors above had louvered shutters.

Dock Street Theatre *(opposite)*

Constructed around 1809 as the Planter's Hotel, the Dock Street Theatre on Church Street is Charleston's last surviving hotel from the antebellum period. Named after the original theatre built in 1736 on Queen Street, the current Georgian-style theatre was reconstructed in the 1930s as a WPA project and seats 464 patrons.

The Joseph Manigault House

Architect Gabriel Manigualt designed
and built this distinguished Adam-style
home in 1803 for his wealthy brother,
Joseph. Originally the family's summer
home, it is now a National Historic Landmark owned by The Charleston Museum.
An exceptional early 19th-century collection of furnishings is on display here.

The Calhoun Mansion

Merchant banker George Walton
Williams built this 24,000-square-foot
Victorian house in 1876 and left it to his
daughter, Mrs. Patrick Calhoun. Elabor-
ately decorated with antiques, it boasts a
stairwell that climbs to a 75-foot domed
ceiling. It is currently the largest private
residence in Charleston.

Sword Gate House

Ironworker Christopher Werner created the elaborate, wrought iron Sword Gate in 1838 for Charleston's New Guard House, but it was not used until about 1849 when it was installed in front of the 32 Legare Street house. The U-shaped mansion boasts the most elegant ball-rooms in the city.

The Wentworth Mansion

The opulent interior of this Second Empire-style mansion has not changed since wealthy cotton merchant Francis Silas Rodgers built it in the 1880s. Guests at this upscale inn enjoy the luxury of America's Gilded Age, surrounded by Tiffany stained-glass windows, marble fireplaces, and hand-carved woodwork.

The Missroon House

Captain James Missroon purchased this East Bay brick home in 1808, and his family occupied it for 50 years. Built in 1789, the house sits at the end of the High Battery boardwalk, where, on April 12, 1861, Charlestonians gathered along the railings to watch the Confederate and Union troops battle at Fort Sumter.

Coates Row

Coates Row is named after Thomas Coates, who built the series of red brick, commercial buildings from 1714 to 1771 across from Rainbow Row. The corner building, which is now a liquor store, housed Harris Tavern. Supposedly, liquor has been sold here uninterrupted since the tavern opened.

St. John's Lutheran Church *(above)*

The classic wrought iron work and the
red door symbolizing the church's early
reference as "the red meeting house"
mark the entrance to St. John's Lutheran
Church. German immigrants held the
first recorded service on May 26, 1734.
The current structure was built in 1817.

Archdale Street's Church Steeples *(opposite)*

The Unitarian Church in Charleston is
the second-oldest church on the peninsula, dating back to 1780. In 1854, architect
Francis D. Lee remodeled the church in
the Gothic Revival style, incorporating
the old church walls into the new design.
The church's cemetery neighbors that of
St. John's Lutheran.

St. John's Lutheran Cemetery *(opposite)*

Time has taken its toll, and these head-stones and monuments in the St. John's Lutheran cemetery are weathered and virtually unreadable. This peaceful ceme-tery is the resting place of Dr. John Bachman, minister of the church from 1815 to 1874 and founder of Newberry College.

French Hugeunot Cemetery *(above)*

Charleston's many cemeteries are tucked next to churches behind stone walls and wrought iron fences. Headstones depict vivid images intricately etched in stone. While the city's first French Huguenot Church and its cemetery date back to 1687, the building seen today was rebuilt in 1844.

The Charleston Museum *(opposite)*

Known as America's oldest museum, founded in 1773, The Charleston Museum chronicles the natural and social history of the city and Lowcountry. Much of its current space is dedicated to trade and commerce, early Native Americans, the plantation system, African-American contributions, and Civil War memorabilia.

CSS H.L. Hunley *(top)*

The CSS *H.L. Hunley*, on display at the Charleston Museum, is a full-size replica of the first submarine in history to sink an enemy ship. On February 17, 1864, the *Hunley* attacked the USS *Housatonic* while it was part of the Union blockade in Charleston Harbor.

Original Museum Columns *(bottom)*

These magnificent column ruins are what remain of the original Charleston Museum, which burned in the late 20th century after the museum moved locations. The columns now stand as a centerpiece of Cannon Park located between Rutledge and Ashley Avenues near Calhoun Street.

The South Carolina Aquarium

Housing over 60 exhibits, the aquarium encourages visitors to learn about the state's diverse aquatic habitats, from mountain streams to salt marshes to the ocean depths. The 93,000-square-foot building houses over 10,000 living organisms, has a variety of interactive exhibits, and a view of the Cooper River.

The Living Wall

The aquarium lobby's 15,000 gallon fish tank is nothing compared to the Great Ocean Tank, which spans the two levels, holds 385,000 gallons of water, and is filled with hammerhead and sand tiger sharks, an array of fish, moray eels, and a loggerhead sea turtle.

Charles Towne Landing

Settled 1670

South Carolina Department of Parks, Recreation and Tourism

A Modern Welcome to History *(top)*

The newly renovated museum and visitor center at Charles Towne Landing has a modern flair. The glass and pine building is part of a seven-year, 19-million-dollar renovation. The revitalized facility was dedicated by South Carolina Governor Mark Sanford and Senior Minister of Barbados, Dame Billie Miller.

Charles Towne Landing *(bottom)*

Charles Towne Landing celebrates the site where the English first settled in 1670. They established what would become the Carolinas colony and one of the continent's first major port cities. The park originally opened in 1970 as part of Charleston's 300th anniversary.

Visitors Center, Charles Towne *(opposite)*

Inside the visitors center is a 12-room interactive museum that includes a digital dig and a self-guided history trail. The trail is enhanced by an MP3 player that adds an audio tour to the experience. The visitor center also provides park information, restrooms, and a gift shop.

Interactive Museum

The Charles Towne Landing's interactive museum allows guests to learn what life was like for the first settlers. Visitors also learn about property disbursement from the Lords Proprietors and indigenous creatures living in the surrounding areas.

Charles Towne Landing Museum

The Charles Towne Landing museum details how the settlers, with their slaves and servants, came together with the local Native Americans to form a community. Eventually, Charles Towne became a major port city and the birthplace of the plantation system for the American South.

Gibbes Museum of Art *(opposite)*

Established in 1905 by the Carolina Art Association, the Gibbes Art Museum houses artwork from the 18th century to the present. The building, located downtown, is a memorial to James Schoolbred Gibbes, a wealthy Charlestonian who donated money to ensure a permanent location for the Association's art collection.

Market Hall *(top)*

The corner of Meeting and Market has been the public market since the late 1700s. Market Hall, completed in 1841, now houses the Confederate Museum operated by the United Daughters of the Confederacy. Vendors line the open-air market behind the building selling sweetgrass baskets and other handmade crafts.

Randolph Hall *(bottom)*

The College of Charleston, America's first municipal college, opened in 1790, but it wasn't until 1828 that construction on the Randolph Hall began. The magnificent Greek revival building overlooks an outdoor cistern, gigantic live oaks, and the lawn where students lounge before class and Spoleto events are held.

Charleston Southern University *(top and bottom)*

Founded in 1964, Charleston Southern University has become one of South Carolina's largest accredited independent universities. The university, whose mission is to promote academic excellence in a Christian environment for all denominations, has built a reputation as a place that allows the student body to develop socially, culturally, spiritually, as well as intellectually. The university sits on 300 gorgeous acres of former rice and indigo plantation and offers more than 33 accredited undergraduate degrees.

Lightsey Chapel *(opposite)*

The Lightsey Chapel Auditorium and Music Building, home to the Summit Church congregation on Sundays, hosts numerous events for both the school and the community during the year, including a concert series and debates. The chapel auditorium, equipped with a modern stage, seats over 1,500 people.

Padgett-Thomas Barracks *(opposite)*

Citadel cadets stand at attention outside the new Padgett-Thomas Barracks, built to resemble the old barracks torn down in 2001. The original building, which had the same name, was the first building on campus after the school relocated to its current location on the Ashley River.

Daniel Library *(top)*

Built in 1960, The Citadel's Daniel Library houses an extensive and impressive collection of books, periodicals, government documents, and pamphlets. The Citadel Museum, located on the first floor of this library, displays the Military College of South Carolina's history from its founding in 1842 to the present.

The Old Citadel *(bottom)*

The Old Citadel, originally the South Carolina State Arsenal, towers over Marion Square. Constructed in the 1830s, the arsenal was soon taken over by the Military Academy. Due to the fortress-like appearance of the building, the Academy became known as The Citadel. It is now a hotel.

The Citadel

Having established a municipal guard for Charleston and surrounding areas, Governor John P. Richardson wanted to incorporate the guard duties with a system of education. On December 20, 1842, the legislature successfully passed such an act. Thus, the Military Academy of South Carolina was born.

The Citadel Band (*above*)

The Regimental Band and Pipes have been a part of The Citadel since 1909 and contribute to daily life at the college. The buglers control the disciplined schedule. The band performs during the Friday dress parade and inspires Citadel athletic teams and fans during games throughout the year.

The Arthur Ravenel Jr. Bridge (*pages 84–85*)

The Ravenel Bridge, which offers the best view of Charleston and Patriots Point in Mount Pleasant, is the third bridge built over the Cooper River in less than 100 years. Prior to August 1929, when the John P. Grace Bridge opened, people were forced to take a ferry.

Cargo Ship

Purposely built for the largest container ships that load and unload in Charleston Harbor, the Ravenel Bridge's main channel clearance is 186 feet high with a 1,576-foot span. Charleston is the second busiest container port on the East Coast.

Cooper River Bridge Run

Every spring, close to 40,000 people participate in the world-famous Cooper River Bridge Run, a 10-kilometer foot race that begins in Mount Pleasant, continues over the Ravenel Bridge, and finishes downtown. The Cooper River Bridge Run is a three-day festival and draws runners from around the world.

Celebrating the Ravenel Bridge *(top and bottom)*

Charleston is a city that knows how to celebrate. For 27 minutes on Thursday, July 14, 2005, 74,000 fireworks lit up the night sky and the new Ravenel Bridge. Patriotic music accompanied the sparkling white, blue, and red bursts of light as thousands of onlookers stood in awe. The fireworks were part of the three-day celebration leading up to the opening of the longest cable-stayed bridge in the Western Hemisphere. After four years of construction, the bridge opened on July 16, 2005, changing the Charleston skyline forever and adding a new chapter to the city's history.

Spoleto Festival USA

The opening ceremony for Spoleto Festival USA is always a colorful event. Beginning Memorial Day weekend, the celebration of visual art, music, opera, dance, and literature continues well into June. The event, which began in 1977, is a time when the city buzzes with excitement and creativity.

Charleston Farmers Market

Every Saturday from April to December, Marion Square buzzes with activity as people flood the Charleston Farmers Market in search of fresh local produce, herbs, and cut flowers. The market is a favorite place for families to gather and listen to live music while shopping.

St. Matthew's Lutheran Church (above)

St. Matthew's Lutheran Church and its 297-foot steeple overlook the bustling Charleston Farmers Market in Marion Square. Designed by architect John Henry Devereaux, the Gothic church was completed in 1872, only to be rebuilt in 1965 after it caught fire.

Drayton Hall (pages 92–93)

Drayton Hall is the oldest example of Georgian Palladian architecture in the United States. The house has held seven generations of the Drayton family, from John Drayton who originally built the home, to Charles and Frank Drayton who sold the property to the National Trust for Historic Preservation in 1974.

Avenue of Live Oaks (*above*)

Controversy surrounds the origin of the
Avenue of Oaks, the famous trees that
line the main drive, but it is widely
believed to have been planted in 1843.
Some say that the Boone family started
the path in 1743, but the majority of
research supports the later date.

Boone Hall Plantation (*opposite*)

The Boone Hall Plantation house was
built in 1936 and is currently owned by
the McRae family. The house remains
open to the public while the property
continues to be farmed.

Historic Cabins *(above and opposite)*

Nine original slave cabins, estimated to have been built between the years of 1790 and 1810, still exist on the Boone Hall Plantation property. While most slave cabins were constructed using wood, these cabins were made of brick. Boone Hall Plantation hosts a Living History Weekend, allowing visitors to travel back in time and experience the lifestyle of the antebellum era. The weekend concludes with a reenactment of The Battle of Secessionville, which includes authentic Civil War reproduction cannons.

Shem Creek (top)

Located in the heart of Mount Pleasant, Shem Creek is home to Charleston's shrimp-boat fleet, playful dolphins, and spectacular sunsets. The deepwater tidal creek derives its name from the Sewee Indian word *Shemee*, and has been an important site for shipbuilding and milling industries since the 1700s.

Twilight at Shem Creek (bottom)

As the sun sets on Shem Creek, lights from the seafood restaurants and local bars are switched on to reveal yet another attraction that the creek has to offer. There is always plenty of dock space to pull up, hop out, and visit one of Mount Pleasant's popular nightlife hotspots.

Kayaks on Shem Creek (opposite)

The deepwater channel known as Shem Creek reflects the colors of the kayaks the same way the water reflects the face of each visitor. Walking along the edge of the dock, the colorful boats call the name of every person that is in need of a little adventure.

Sunset on Ashley River

As the sun sets on the Ashley River, the water continues to flow out from South Carolina until it meets the Atlantic Ocean. The yellow sun surrounds itself with different shades of orange as the light fades from the sky, and the lighthouse begins its nightly duty.

Dunes West Golf Club

The Dunes West Golf Club is located on the site of the historic Lexington Planta-tion in Mount Pleasant. Bermuda-covered dunes are accented with 200-year-old live oaks draped in Spanish moss. The slow-moving waterways that flow along the edge of the green are reminders that this is still the Lowcountry.

The USS Yorktown (top)

The USS *Yorktown* was named for the only American carrier lost in the Battle of Midway. The ship has a rich history that includes being launched by First Lady Eleanor Roosevelt, being a target of Japan's Kamikaze missions, and then earning the Presidential Unit Citation for extraordinary acts of heroism.

USS Yorktown Flight Deck (bottom)

Helicopters and planes, on display for visitors, sit on the flight deck of the 900-foot ship affectionately called "The Fighting Lady" by her 2,500-member crew. An Essex class carrier, the *Yorktown* was longer, wider, and heavier than all preceding aircraft carriers, thus positioning herself as the backbone of the Navy.

The James B. Edwards Bridge (opposite)

The I-526 James B. Edwards Bridge, which crosses over the Wando River, was built in 1988 with pre-cast concrete segments. The bridge was named for former South Carolina Governor James B. Edwards.

Sullivan's Island Lighthouse (*opposite*)

Sullivan's Island Lighthouse was built in 1962 due to concern for the quickly eroding Morris Island Lighthouse. It may not have a traditional lighthouse image, but it is the first American lighthouse equipped with air conditioning and an elevator for the lighthouse keeper.

The Pride of Charleston (*above*)

Modeled to resemble the old coastal schooners from Charleston's past, the 84-foot Tall Ship's large sails fill with wind as the boat moves out to sea. Whether visitors choose daytime or sunset cruises, a sail on the *Pride* offers a tour of the harbor that can never be replicated from the mainland.

Isle of Palms (*above*)

With six miles of pristine beaches, there is plenty of room for everyone to play in the Atlantic's rolling waves off the Isle of Palms. A Mount Pleasant barrier island, it is a popular resort and residential island, featuring palm-lined boulevards with stately, colorful homes, fine dining, and rooftop bars.

Sullivan's Island Lighthouse (*opposite*)

Made of aluminum paneling and anchored by steel girders to withstand severe hurricanes, the candlepower of this 163-foot lighthouse is so intense that ships can see it beyond American waters. Sullivan's Island Lighthouse is currently active and not open to the public.

Beach Driftwood

The city of Charleston is a short drive from beautiful salt marshes, miles of pristine beaches, and acres of lush forest that exist along the Atlantic Coast. The Seabrook Island Resort, an hour drive from the city, is a private 2,200-acre island that includes vacation villas, cottages, and private homes.

Sunset on the Docks

There is nothing more spectacular than the sunsets over Charleston and its coast, especially when sailboats and yachts are in the foreground. Beautiful colors of orange, pink, and red linger in the sky long after the sun has gone down.

Isle of Palms Pier

The Isle of Palms Pier, a favorite place for visitors who stay on the beachfront, jets out into the Atlantic. For a small island, there is plenty to do, including volleyball, tennis, boating, crabbing, and shopping. Wild Dunes Resort, on the northern end, features a golf course designed by Tom Fazio.

Ellis Creek

Private boat docks nestled among reeds of grass are a common sight along Ellis Creek on James Island. The creek, named after the Thomas Baynard Ellis family, provides a view of downtown Charleston and, in the distance, the Ravenel Bridge.

Edwin S. Taylor Pier (*above*)

The Folly Beach Edwin S. Taylor Pier is 24 feet wide, extends 1,045 feet into the Atlantic Ocean, and stands 23 feet above sea level. A short drive from downtown Charleston, families enjoy many activities such as fishing, birding, and walking. The pier offers the best views of Folly Beach.

Folly Beach Pier (*opposite*)

After extensive renovations and much anticipation, Folly Beach Pier reopened in March of 2008. The new pier offers restaurants, restrooms, a 1,400-square-foot covered shelter, and a gift and tackle shop. Annual fishing tournaments and dances are held here.

Kiawah Island (*pages 114–115*)

Twenty-one miles from Charleston, Kiawah is a golf haven with five public courses and two private. Named for the Kiawah Native Americans who inhabited the island up to the 1600s, Kiawah Island is perfectly situated between the Atlantic Ocean and lush marshes of the mainland.

Net Casting for Shrimp (top)

A local fisherman casts his shrimping net. Net fishing for shrimp is popular among Charleston residents. Shrimp is a major product in Lowcountry waters where the season begins in spring and ends in the late fall.

Lowcountry Birds (bottom)

The Lowcountry offers great opportunities for bird and wildlife watching, as the coastal area between the city of Charleston and St. Marys is on the Atlantic flyway. With nine national wildlife refuges and several state-owned sanctuaries, these birds have plenty of space to live with only the occasional curious viewer.

Coastal Green Spaces (opposite)

Charleston County has some of the largest numbers of salt marshes in South Carolina, since numerous marshes and swamps drain along the basins of the coastal rivers. Many areas in the Lowcountry have been designated national wildlife refuges to preserve the coastal marshland of the state.

Lowcountry Marsh and Dock

Private docks built among the grass species known as cordgrass, by far the dominant plant in the saltwater marshes, is a common sight in the Charleston area. South Carolina has almost 400,000 acres of coastal marshes and 100,000 acres of tidal swamps.

Trees by the Marsh (*above*)

The numerous marshes throughout the Lowcountry make for postcard-perfect moments, when the breeze is just right and the only noise is from nature. The marshes themselves are wetlands, similar to swamps, but the major difference is swamps have more trees and bushes.

The Scenic Lowcountry (*pages 120–121*)

The South Carolina marshes supply nutrients to many different types of fish. Croaker, drum, flounder, kingfish, menhaden, mullet, and spot are all fish that benefit from the heavy marshes that pepper the Lowcountry. Marshes also serve as grazing areas for horses and cattle.

Lowcountry Marsh

The beauty of the South Carolina Lowcountry is available to any visitor of the marsh. The lush green grasses mix with the tall, curved trees as they reach up to reveal clouds that beg to be viewed and reinterpreted by an imagination at work.

Stillness on the Marsh

The colors that the salt marshes offer visitors never hold themselves back from breaking conventional ideas. When the sun bathes the grass at different times of the year, the marshes mix oranges in with the green grasses, which both jump from the ground and meet the blue sky.

Lowcountry Serenity

As the sun falls on the marsh each day,
it is almost as if time begins to slow as
well. The water grows still, and the
trees and grass relax as the breeze
lessens. After a long day of standing
bright with the sun, the lush vegetation
glows a little softer.

Sunbathed Marsh

The Lowcountry sun has a unique ability to apply itself to the marsh. Long rows of South Carolina vegetation stretch out to absorb a sun that is always welcome. Like a cat on its back soaking up the sun, the marsh brings the light home from every angle.

Lowcountry Salt Marshes

In the months of April and May, higher tides offer excellent opportunities to fish for red drum in the breathtaking marsh flats. Often, anglers will exit the boat and wade into the shallows in search of the perfect catch.

Cruising the Marsh

The many water trails that open themselves up for boats to glide along are invitations to adventures. The blue water and the blue sky of the Lowcountry explain why so many have dropped anchor and declared themselves home.

Rick Rhodes has a passion for what he does. Whether soaring at 1500 feet above Charleston's Harbor, riding to the very top of the spectacular new span of the Arthur Ravenel Bridge, or with his feet firmly planted on the ground, Rick's photography of his native Charleston shares a personal admiration for the region.

Born and raised in Charleston, South Carolina, Rick first began taking photos on the playground and later expanded to the dark room in high school. He pursued his formal education at the Southeast Center for Photographic Studies in Daytona Beach, Florida and Brooks Institute of Photography in Santa Barbara, California earning degrees in Commercial Photography and Color Technology.

Rick uses his creative eye along with his extensive technical talents to capture commercial or nature subjects and communicate through them. His favorite work continues to be using his 4 x 5 camera to photograph architecture and landscapes.

Rick Rhodes Photography is his commercial photography studio in the West Ashley area of Charleston. To view more of Rick's work, visit his website at www.rickrhodesphotography.com.

Photograph of Rick Rhodes by Elise Poche

Michelle Salater is an award-winning freelance travel writer and owner of a copywriting company specializing in travel marketing. She resides in Charleston, South Carolina, and has written extensively of the city she loves and now calls home. To view more of Michelle's work, visit www.mlsalater.com